JOURNEY OF THE WIND

by TOMIHIRO HOSHINO

Translated by
KYOKO & GAVIN BANTOCK

RIPPU

FOREWORD

I am very happy to begin a new journey to faraway places by means of the brush held in my mouth.

The winter mountains are ranged before me. Covered with the fallen leaves of trees, they are warm-coloured like the tail of a squirrel. Perhaps this is Nature's consolation to us in the cold weather.

In my boyhood, I was not very fond of these mountains. I couldn't bear the thought of living such a mountain life——working in the narrow fields, like my parents, my hands covered with earth.

At the first glance, money and social position seem to make people happy. Maybe I used to think that such things were beyond the mountains.... "Some day... surely some day I will find them...."

I remember gazing at the mountains with such thoughts. In June of the year of my graduation from university, however, that "Some day..." attacked me in a totally unexpected way.

In 1970, without any warning an accident happened in the gymnasium of the school where I was working. I tried to turn a somersault, failed, and fell to the floor. My pupils thought I had done it as a joke as usual.

It seems to be an ability of the human mind that people can remember past pain with joy later.

Looking back on my nine years of hospital life, I remember the encouragement of the nurses and my friends rather than any hardship, the warm letters of my pupils rather than sorrow, the flowers near the window rather than the ceiling of the hospital. I was strongly impressed by the word "Live!"——from my mother or from the Bible, rather than by my own idea——"Let me die".

Now the same mountains I gazed at in my boyhood are before me. Here is my home village with its winding pathways, and in the fields

at the foot of the mountains, farmers are doggedly at work, bent close to the ground like stones.

The shadow of the wheel of my wheel-chair is getting bigger like a rainbow. The distant tinkle of a music box from the Primary School is floating in the air. The evening sun is sinking low, dyeing the mountains, the trees and myself all the same colour.

The darkness of night makes the morning brighter. We often realize the value of things after we have lost them. People move their fingers unintentionally, and walk naturally on their two legs as a matter of course. But there are more important matters than these visible things.

Maybe "To lose" and "To be given" are next-door neighbours.

My dream "Some day..." is not an encounter with success in life or being promoted to a high position——which I dreamed of in my boyhood. I had the illusion that I could live by my own power alone; the reality is this: my existence is very small, but it encounters great love. And I think now that such a wonderful encounter as this is worth more than anything else in the world.

TOMIHIRO HOSHINO

CONTENTS

I BROKEN RAPE BLOSSOMS

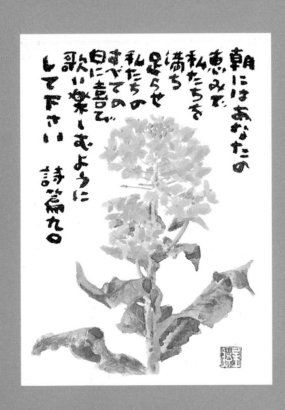

朝にはあなたの
恵みで私たちを
満ち
足らせ
私たちの
すべての
日に喜で
歌い楽しむように
して下さい　詩篇九○

Pushing my wheel-chair under a cherry tree
my friend pulled down a branch in full bloom
burying my face in blossoms

With a surge of ungovernable joy
I bit off a mouthful of blossom
eating the pink-white petals
munching and munching

Cherry Blossoms (1977)

When you came in so gently
   all of us in that room
   gazed with dreamy eyes
   at your pure white dress

   When I said to you
      Nurse
   you look like a gardenia

You let out a squeak and fled

   (*What a big mouth she has !*)

Why
with your roots sunk deep in black soil
and drinking muddy water
do you bloom so beautifully?

And why do I
with so many loving people all around me
think such ugly thoughts?

Japanese Iris (1978)

A man who can walk
needs patience to stay in one place

A man like me who cannot
seems not to need it

Suddenly
understanding this
I knew the rope of thorns
tightly binding my body
had vanished

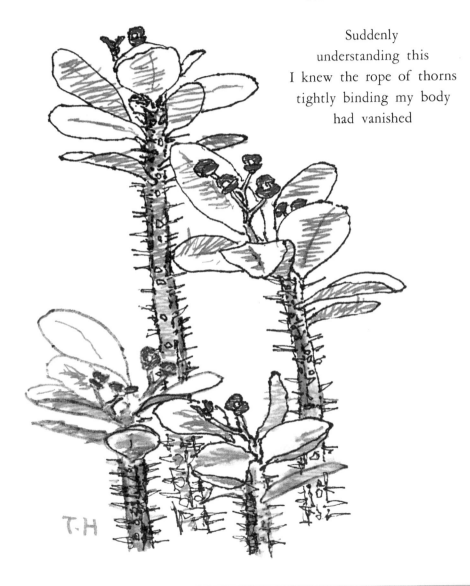

Thorn Flower (1974)

The stalk broken easily
like my neck

Yet
in that very place
new buds appear
fresh blossoms

Like this flower
I drink water

I enjoy the same sunlight

I will grow strong

With my poor brush-work
I can't paint even a thousandth
part of this flower's beauty

But I want to keep it
forever in my heart

Mr. N took great pains
to grow this flower
then cutting off the entire stem
presented it to me

I want to keep this flower
and his kind heart
forever blooming in my mind

Orchid (1975)

You placed an azalea
between my fingers
didn't you?

You stuck another
in the shoe of your artificial leg

Without words you said
Never give up
didn't you?

How are you now?

I'd like to tell you
those red flowers are blooming again
this year too

In the morning light
through the window-blind
the second bloom
parted into six petals
each quietly curling back

Watching this slow miracle
I felt it would be arrogant
to paint this flower

May I paint you, lily?

Iris (1975)

II   TO FLOWERS

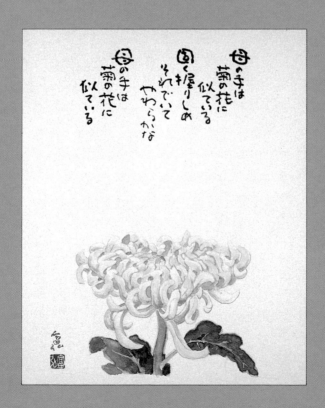

母の手は
菊の花に
似ている
固く握りしめ
それでいて
やわらかな
母の手は
菊の花に
似ている

Using my dictionary,　I wrote you a letter,
memorizing some complex Chinese characters.

I never think about you now,
but I can never forget the characters I learned then.

The characters for *butterbur*,　*pretty*,
rose and *melancholy*——
they all have complex strokes——like your heart.

I have seen you flying in the sky
When was it?

Your way of travelling
fills me with joy

You each carry only one thing
on the wind

It is the only thing necessary
for human beings

If I could throw away what I don't need
even I could fly in the sky

If something is true
many words are not necessary

There is something bright in a tiny gesture
like wild grass
trembling in the wind

Asters (1980)

A flower doesn't know her own prettiness
so she can bloom beautifully

Or,   I wonder,
does she know her own prettiness
and can therefore bloom with beauty?

Flowers bloom facing upwards

I am lying on my back,　face up

Both these seem quite natural
but in them I can feel
God's deep love

Your flowers,   blooming in clusters,
seem to be cheerful

But each flower has a sad face

It is just the same with human beings

Camellia flowers,   I hear,
drop down like severed heads

People say that under cherry trees
dead bodies are buried

Gold-banded lilies,   I hear,
like the sound of people moaning

People say that the spider lily
blooms best in grave-yards

Flowers,   beautiful as you are,
why is death so near you?

What are the bonds between beauty
and human life?

Your tender stalk is easily broken
with one light tap

God has given your flower
the shape and colour of a viper's head
to protect you from people
who might try to pick you

In Autumn,   unseemly as you are,
you bear crimson berries

God creates everything

I,   too,
with this poor body of mine
will rejoice

Some people pick you carefully
Others call you "smelly"
and say you are a nuisance

But you live quietly
at the corner of the path
gazing at people's legs as they walk past

You look as if you are waiting
for someone who needs you

Your flower resembles a white cross

Fulfilling its duty
one of your flowers is about to drop off
but just beside it
a new bud is about to open

Even one of your branches
reveals to us
the entire scheme of nature

Camellia (1978)

Some intertwined
some climbing up towards the sky
some drooping with resignation

Your petals are waves of the sea
attacking a quay-side

When waves draw far back
they gather with greater power
returning with violence

Chrysanthemum (1979)

A tree cannot move by itself

With all its might
it spreads its branches wide
trying to achieve its ordained height
with utmost effort
in that one place on earth
given to it by God

Such trees,   I feel,
are my friends

Camellias (1979)

Your pale flower reminds me of
Mother
weakness and sorrow
combining in one warm colour
reminding me of
Mother

A mother's hand is like
a chrysanthemum
clenched hard,   but soft

Yes,
a chrysanthemum
is like a mother's hand

Chrysanthemum (1977)

If God would allow me to move my arm
only once
I'd like to pat and thump my mother on the shoulder
to ease her pain

Gazing at the seed-pods of Mother's-Heart
I know that sooner or later
such a day will come

Mother's-Heart (1979)

III TRACES OF THE WIND

一本の甘草が
一本の棒を登って行く
棒の先には夏の空
私も あんなふうに 登って行きたい

I felt someone was looking at me

I turned my wheel-chair

A small flower was blooming there

What a marvellous day!

Beyond the azaleas
an old man is walking

Carrying a baby on his back
and walking with light steps

Right leg   Left leg
Right   Left

Oh!   now he's standing on one leg
Ah!   and twisting in a half-turn

What a remarkable thing!
A human being is walking

Before
I too used to do such wonderful things
without a care in the world

I was injured

But now
your kindness enters the wound
and touches my heart

I can speak to other people
only trivial things

I can't bear the frustration
of not being able to say
what I want to say most

Maybe
I paint pictures or sing songs
in order to say what I want to say

Maybe
I long for someone

My mother is weeding
grumbling at the weeds

She must be happy to be doing that
pulling up thick clumps of grass
her hands all muddy
and the sweat running down
although
she never stops grumbling

She must be glad
to be standing on the soft earth again

I do not need a wedding ring,   you said,

When I wash your face in the morning
it might hurt you
and I don't want to hurt you
when I lift you up

No,   you said,
I do not need a wedding ring

*

Morning light
filters through the lace curtain

You are my wife now

You scoop up water from the washbowl

The drops of water
falling from your ten fingers
are more beautiful
than
silver or gold

One tendril climbs up a single stick

At the top of the stick is the summer sky

I wish I could climb up like that

Joy has a short life

Sorrow,   too,   is a tiny flash
if I see it in the bright light of day

In the morning garden
I found a small cold blob
dropped from a child's firework

Once
looking at some flowering weeds
trembling in the breeze
I sensed their weakness

Today
seeing the same weeds
trembling in the breeze
I realize their strength

Tawny Day Lily (1980)

A boy is running
from the other side of my memory

It might be me
wearing for the first time ever
white sports shoes
given to me that very day

The wetness of crushed weeds
staining his white shoes
he is running towards the present
with such joy on his face!

My mother used to spend all day
weeding in the fields of the farm
feeding the silkworms with mulberry leaves
and in the evening
popping outside to pick some Japanese ginger
selling it,   and buying some pickles for my lunch box
——always salty seaweed boiled in soy......

I remember
she picked off the flowers before selling them
(with the flowers on they sold more cheaply)
her bare ankles covered with mosquito bites

Mother,
although people say eating Japanese ginger
makes us absent minded,
I remember many things

The day I changed into my winter school-uniform
I was touched by a faint tenderness

The scent of camphor-balls......

My mother's kimono had the same smell......

She came to watch our athletic meeting
wearing her best kimono......

Clusters of sorrow
I feel
are closer to real happiness
than clusters of joy

Crowds of weak people
I feel
are closer to truth
than crowds of strong people

Clusters of unhappiness
I feel
are closer to love
than clusters of happiness

Chrysanthemums (1981)

For one flower to bloom
how many leaves
I wonder
must endure the winter's cold?

Camellia leaves are shining
polished by the winter wind

They shine like Mother

Human beings sleep on their backs
facing the sky

Facing the sky with sorrow
facing the sky with weariness
facing the sky with victory

When we are ill
when we go to bed at the end of day
God makes us turn our faces up
towards the infinite sky

God,   are you telling us
to gaze at eternity?

Human beings sleep on their backs
facing the sky

Evergreen Magnolia (1979)

IV   RANDOM THOUGHTS

NOTES FROM A SICKBED

14 APRIL, 1973

I was thinking that when Spring came, I'd be able to go outside and do lots of new things.

Well, Spring *has* come now——the grass is growing and the cherry blossoms have opened: we can bare our breasts at open windows and breathe deeply.

Come on, now's the time!

It's no good sighing with disappointment because I can't do anything except gaze at the beauty of flowers.

15 APRIL

My friend came to see me. I wanted to show him a big cheerful face; I wanted to tell him I was getting stronger.

I suddenly found I was talking about the cherry blossom opening and my home town.

16 APRIL

Many sparrows were flying in the cloudy sky today. I haven't seen the sky for a long time. I've been lying on my back all the time. I wonder what on earth I've been looking at.

17 APRIL

Went outside today.
There was nothing there but fresh grass,
budding flowers and sprouting leaves.
Nothing but new life.
Nothing but living things growing up.
"God who gives us Life ——
I went outside today!"

*

My mother pushed my bed-on-wheels out into the back garden of the hospital.

Cottonweed flowers seemed to be leaning towards the ruin of a concrete wall destroyed in a fire.

I looked up into the sky as the flowers did. The light was so bright I felt tears in my eyes.

I was ashamed because my mother thought I was crying.

*

Lying on my back, I spoke ill of others.

From the corner of my right eye, I caught sight of the peach blossoms opening with a smile.

*

Some parts of my body laugh at other people's unhappiness.

I am frustrated by other people's happiness.

If I feel even slightly irritated by someone, I often think: "I hope he'll become a paralytic like me."

I find that ugly thoughts hiding in the corners of my heart get bigger and bigger.

Does this....jaundiced mind of mine, I wonder, come from my disabled body?

I'm in the wrong, I know, but I can't forgive others, and this becomes a pain growing bigger and bigger——much greater than the pain of not being able to move my arms and legs.

Only when looking at flowers and facing a piece of white paper can I escape from that pain.

*

Sweet-smelling winter daphne is opening quietly in a nook of the garden.

I must take great care to paint even the tiniest of its petals.

*

They measured my weight today.

The doctor, holding me in arms, stepped onto the weighing machine——

105 kilograms.

His weight is 70....

How light I am!

*

One of my friends brought me a potted azalea.

"When the flowers are finished," he said, "I'll take it back home, and next year, when the flowers open again, I'll lend it to you again."

That means that during the time it has no flowers he must water it every day and take care of it.

How poorly I repay him for his promise! I've never done anything like that for him.

*

With my mother, I watched the sunset through the ginkgo tree for a long time.

Every day, beside the same bench, we see the days lengthening, as if Happiness is coming nearer and nearer. This makes me happy.

Back in my sickroom, I found some sweet-smelling winter daphne in my vase.

*

Mr. T used to take me for a walk in my wheel-chair. He was good at juggling and a clever mimic. He always kept everybody in the ward laughing.

On the day he left hospital, I went with my mother to the entrance hall. As he walked through the heavy rain to his car, he looked back often, bowing many times.

I also bowed my head often, though I can't move it very much.

Mr. T waved his hand from his car. I couldn't wave my hand, so I wagged my tongue from left to right.

I had given him my "Iris" picture. I watched his car fade into the distance.

*

For six years, Mr. K has been bringing me flowers in hospital.

The flowers——which he grows himself——are as tough as weeds, and sometimes I notice insects crawling on them. I love these flowers. Once I noticed the imprint of his fingers in the newspaper he wrapped the flowers in. He must have carried them a great distance.

A SINGLE STAR

I've got a bald patch on the back of my head.   It's about as big as a ten-yen coin.

When I was first injured, I had to lie on my back for several months.

I got a bed-sore on the back of my head; the skin came off, and a bald patch developed.

I used to have no mark anywhere on my head (though my brain is full of flaws!). Since I got this bald patch, I've been feeling anxious.

I worried that the man in the next bed could see my bald patch when I lay on my side.

It has been my companion for a long time, and now I find it unexpectedly helpful sometimes.

If someone touches me anywhere below my neck, I can feel nothing; but above my neck my nerves are still alive, and the whole surface of my head is ultra-sensitive, as if all the nerves of my body have gathered there.

Whenever I thought about my head, it felt itchy all the time; but I couldn't move my hand to scratch it.   I asked my mother to scratch my head for me, but she couldn't find the place where it tickled.

Although I said "At the top" or "At the side", because there are no lines of division on my head, she still couldn't find the place; so I had the idea of using my bald patch as a landmark to help her.   At first, I felt ashamed to mention the existence of my bald patch to my mother and room-mates; but at last I said: "Mother, I feel itchy above my bald patch!"   She immediately found the right place.

Since then, I've often referred to it——"At the side of my bald patch"...."Between my ear and the bald patch"....so now it's easy to pin-point my itchy places, because my bald patch is like a town centre surrounded by streets and blocks.

Twinkling like a single star in the black sky of my hair, that bald patch of mine is doing fine!

WATARASE RIVER

In my childhood, the River Watarase, flowing near my house, taught me many things.

I think it was in my primary-school days that I first learned how to swim.

Our ring-leader took us to the river as usual. The level had risen that day, and the water was muddy.

The current was swift. The bigger boys could swim across to the opposite bank; but I was only a beginner, and with my dogpaddle played in the shallow water near the bank, sometimes venturing out into the middle of the fast-flowing stream and coming back again.

Once, without knowing, I swam beyond the centre-point, and suddenly realized I was caught in the strong current.

I tried hard to swim back to the bank, but the stream rushed faster and faster. All my friends were soon out of sight.

Paddling my hands and feet desperately, I struggled to swim back against the current; but the river carried me along at breakneck speed, and crying out for help I swallowed gallons of water.

Stories of children drowning flooded into my mind. At the same time, an idea came like a flash.

I remembered the way the water flowed in the River Watarase, which I had so often gazed at.

I remembered that one part of the stream was deep blue water; the other part, bubbling white, was only knee-deep.

I was out of my depths and almost drowning; but suddenly I knew that if I followed the stream, sooner or later I'd come to a shallow place.

The place where I had been playing before was not the only shallow part of the river.

"....Yes, I see....I needn't try to swim back...."

I made a hundred-and-eighty-degree turn and began to swim down with the stream. The terrifying speed and high waves which were swallowing me up quietened down, and the stream once again was the same River Watarase, which I gazed at every day....

After drifting for a while, I tried to touch the bottom with my feet. To my surprise, the water was no more than thigh-deep.

My joy in escaping from the strong stream was ten times greater than my terrible fear....

When I was worrying about my future and thinking about my past days——and knew that since I injured myself I could not move——I suddenly saw in my mind's eye my own figure struggling against the strong current to get back to the bank where I had started swimming....

And then I thought: "I needn't go back there: flowing with the stream, I can just go along with it, doing whatever I can."

Till then, I had been completely controlled by my consciousness of struggling against my injury; but at that moment, I felt it gradually fading away.

Faced with total paralysis of hands and feet, I had fought through each day with set teeth; but from that moment I decided that from now on I would live, learning from my paralyzed body....

I read in the painter Kaii Higashiyama's book that in his childhood he had a similar experience to mine——in the sea. It gave me a strong impression, and I suddenly recalled a saying from the Bible I had come across some time before:

"There hath no temptation taken you but such as man can bear: but God is faithful, who will not suffer you to be tempted above that ye are able; but will with the temptation make also the way of escape, that ye may be able to endure it."

(Corinthians I, Chapter 10, Verse 13)

PICTURE OF ORCHIDS

One of my friends was surprised to find that my writing by mouth was no different from my handwriting.

The characteristics of my handwriting were conveyed to my writing by mouth. Even I think this is strange. On second thoughts, both hand and mouth are moved by the same inner personality, so I suppose the similarity is quite natural——even though it seems like a miracle to me. When I discovered this "miracle", I felt a new hope ——to start painting pictures by mouth.

I thought that if beauty could still move my heart, even I could somehow express it in pictures.

This orchid picture on page 13 is my first complete picture painted by mouth.

At that time, my neck was so weak that even to draw a single line on the paper felt as if I were dragging a heavy object.

That's why this is my most memorable work.

Looking at the background lines which took me three days to do with a felt-tipped pen, I remember everything about that time as clearly as reading a diary.

As I drew the first line, another saying from the Bible came into my mind:

"Do all things without murmurings and disputings."
(Philippans, Chapter 2, Verse 14)

Taking the first step in great agony, I felt utterly forlorn; but.... maybe, I thought, a new world beyond my imagination would be revealed. Painting a picture by mouth was, I felt, like the first step.

Drawing each background line, almost drained of strength I dribbled at the mouth; but, one by one, the orchids stood out vividly. It was not only a picture, but a hopeful light in my heart.

To be injured as I am is not entirely a minus. Looking at my first picture, I am sure of this.

My mother, who has taken such good care of me since I entered hospital, will, I am sure, feel the same.

FLOWERS

When I begin to draw a flower, I like my heart to be as pure and white as the drawing paper.

If I look carefully, even at flowers of the same kind, I see that each has its own personality, just as people have different faces. It also sometimes happens that a flower of the morning will have changed its colour a little by the evening.

By looking at a flower often, I have a pre-conceived idea what it looks like ("This flower must have a shape like this"), but when I begin to draw the flower, it sometimes turns away its face....

Flowers which are open too wide cannot be sold in the shops. The flowers are too far open and the pistils and stamens too much exposed. Sometimes, however, I think they are shockingly beautiful in this condition.

Flowers that have lost a petal or two or have been nibbled at by insects are quite attractive; and so are finished flowers, their petals turning brown....

It doesn't mean the flower is dead. Its afterlife is its finest hour, for then the fruit begins to grow.

On the other hand, some of them are broken by the wind and hang down, and some of them are warped with illness or some other affliction.

Some flowers bloom powerfully in sunny places. Some of them get dirty near the roots as the rain splashes earth upon them.

As I look at them, they appear to me just like human beings in society. Some of them are clever, some are not; some are beautiful, some not so; some are ill, some healthy. So many different kind of people exist in the world!

I myself, however, quite often decide that "that fellow is that kind of man"——without knowing him well.

The colour of a flower can change within one day. Looking at people with minds and hearts, we are wrong to measure them with our own little minds.

A magnificent large chrysanthemun is blooming before my eyes.

Chrysanthemums bloom for quite a long time, and people admire them, but even this period is short compared with the long life of the plant itself.

When I paint the petals of a flower, I wish to express the beauty of the leaves *under* the flower, *and* the far-down beauty of the roots deep in the earth....

GOING BACK HOME

For me, after a long time in hospital, greeting the Spring in my hometown is a special delight——the verandah filled with sunlight, with the washing above it swinging gently in the breeze, the cat sharpening its claws on the wooden pillar....

The beauty of a thousand ordinary things merging slowly into one great whole called "everyday life"....the beauty passes abundantly before my eyes each day.... Somehow I feel this is the first spring I've ever spent in my hometown.

Listening to the sound of the whispering leaves in the bamboo groves, I draw a picture.... In no time at all the morning passes by.

In the afternoon, I take a ride in my special-order wheelchair, which I can operate with my neck....going out into the garden alone, taking a walk along the narrow path.

It's most enjoyable for me to go outside now; I've been inside the house right through the winter.

It's so refreshing to see the plum blossom and camellias blooming on actual trees rooted in the earth, and not in flower vases....

Not many people grow Chinese Milk Vetch or Rape Blossoms nowadays, so I can't see many; but there are still thousands of wild flowers growing strongly everywhere.

I want to fill my sketch-book full with my hometown flowers....

HOME TOWN

At three o'clock in the afternoon, my mother and sister-in-law carry me from bed to my wheel-chair. They say I'm getting a bit heavier lately.

In case I should meet a beautiful lady while out for a ride, I comb my untidy hair, fasten my seat-belt, and adjust my rearview mirror ——getting everything ready before I set out.

My driving ability in this electric-chair of mine is improving. I can go out by myself now.

As I go down the slope, a beautiful lady....a lady snake——more than beautiful with her head one twentieth of her total length—— often crosses my path, glancing up sideways at me.

Of course, a pedestrian has right of way, so I'm willing to wait, with a sort of creepy excitement, till her slender tail is hidden in the grass.

Turning the corner of the stone wall, I drive at the amazing speed of four kilometres an hour. A dragon-fly overtakes me, passing effortlessly. Beyond the green tunnel of the lane, I can catch the smell of manure. I often pause here a while, lost in thought....

Because of their sense of smell, I've heard, salmon can return to their home rivers. Each person has a special smell he can never forget. In my case, the sight of acacia always reminds me of the smell of toilets.

Just below the road on the way to my primary school, there was an acacia tree, and near it was a toilet.

After a long while in hospital, when I first came out of my room into the corridor and smelt the same smell in front of the toilet, I felt full of joy to realize that I had survived, that I was still alive....

Although there is a great difference between the smell of manure and a toilet, the smell of toilets is for me one of the flavours of my home town.

My small village seems to be buried in an abundance of growing greenness.

The breeze climbs up the summer hill leaving silver footsteps as it lifts the leaves of trees.

It is almost the time of the year to hear the cheerful sound of the bamboo flute and hand-drum echoing in the mountains.

The sound of evening cicadas seems to float down from the fading sky. When they stop singing, people begin to practise for the Yagi-bushi Bon-dance.

AZUMA VILLAGE

On fine days, I sometimes go to look at the Watarase River near my house.

The gravel track I used to take to my primary school is a main road now, with a tarmacked footpath for the children to walk on.

I went a little way down the slope near Taro Shrine.

Far down——through the footrest of my wheel-chair——the white shingle of the river-bed caught my eye.

The Watarase River winds her way, twisting and looping at her pleasure through the wide shingle of her bed. There is too little water, leaving here and there shoals, which I see bubbling white, and hearing the light sound of the meagre stream, I know the river down there is running.

Above the white shingles of the river, there are several terraces of land, and directly from there a mountain almost a thousand metres high rises straight up.

People find places between the river and the mountain, and build their houses there, tilling their small fields.

The main road and the railway line follow the contours of the mountain and the river's twists and loops, in gentle curves.

High up is the mountain; down below——the river.

The people of the village are living peacefully in the crook of Nature's arm, who never sneezes or turns over in her sleep, but lies there quietly all the while.

When the pink azaleas open on the cliffs above the River Watarase, the village people, following an age-old custom, plant their *taro*-potatoes, knowing the best time for this from the flowering of the azaleas. The dates on a calendar cannot show us the climate of the year, so now these flowers have a special name——"*Taro*-planting azaleas".

These "*Taro*" azaleas open tree by tree up the mountain ridge——as a sign of Spring's arrival.

Now Spring has truly come to Azuma Village. Spring water, bits of dry grass floating on the surface, flows in the rice-field channels, and here and there mechanical cultivators clatter at their work.

The water in the rice-fields reflects the mountain and azaleas.

People from the town cry "What beautiful scenery!"——and the

village people, hearing these words, look up wide-eyed at the mountain——as if for the first time, because they themselves, living merged within that landscape, don't know the beauty of their own hometown.

People call my little village *Shuku*, or *Stage-Town*. In the old days, copper from Ashio Copper Mine was carried this way, and people named the road Copper Road. Our village was one of the stages on the route, and the name *Shuku* is a reminder of those days.

At the side of the road stand many houses, which even now people call by their former inn or shop names——Tamaki-ya, Konishi-ya, Tomi-ya, Tama-ya, Sumiyoshi-ya, and so on. I also used only these old trade names in my childhood. Even now I don't know the real family names of most of the occupants.

They used to come up the River Watarase and climb the twisting road to Ashio Copper Mine, returning the same way.

My village at the top of its slope was, I think, one of their stopping places —— a place where they could catch their breath.

THE CRYING MOUNTAIN

One day my nephew visited me. He was wearing a digital watch. Knowing it was quite the latest style of watch, I was surprised to see this third-year pupil of primary school wearing one with such a casual air. And then I began to wonder what age I was when I first had a watch of my own.

Behind my house is a mountain ridge called Nako Mountain. Even when I was a child people called it that, so I didn't think anything of it; but, according to my mother, the name means "Weeping Ridge" or "Crying Mountain".

Nowadays, even in the mountain villages, everyone uses gas or oil for heating and cooking, though a few houses still burn wood, but only to heat up their bath-water. About fifteen or sixteen years ago, every house had a stack of firewood piled high under the eaves. Each house had a wood-burning stove in the kitchen and an open hearth sunk in the floor of the living room, and smoke came out of the roof-chimney. Collecting firewood for the year was an important job in winter for the wives and children.

The mountainside nearest the houses was completely cleared of dead branches as if it had been swept with a brush. People usually had to climb right over into the next valley and gather wood from the mountainsides there. When I was at primary school, in the winter vacations I also went over the mountain twice a day collecting wood with the neighbourhood children, bringing it home on my back. If I stayed at home and everybody else went to the mountain, there was no one to play with. Going to the mountain was more fun. As I grew stronger and my bundle of sticks got bigger, I was happy to think I was growing up into an adult, like the bundle of sticks itself.

The hardest part was climbing back over the mountain ridge loaded with firewood. As we crossed the stepping-stones over the river where hill trout lived we chatted gaily and sang out of tune; but as we went up the slope we could only breathe out white breath through clenched teeth. Everybody took as much wood as he could carry over the mountain. The last ten yards was the worst of all: the slope was almost vertical. On the rock at the top of the ridge, the sweat dripping off those in front of me made marks like rain. Our arms were numb and our guts were squeezed tight with pain.

The name Crying Mountain comes from the idea of people crying or even dying of the pain of that hard climb. My father and mother, and their mothers too——everybody knew the agony of climbing that slope with panting breaths.... but they chose to cry rather than to die. The actual distance is not very great but the climb is so hard that it seems a whole day is concentrated into one moment. Our steps got smaller and smaller, and words like "I'm done for" somehow escaped from our bodies. Suddenly....bright light in front of our eyes. We had reached the top of the ridge!

The bright south-facing slope was a comfortable place to rest. The rocks and lie of the land, after long use, gradually formed themselves into natural chairs. We sat there and stretched our legs, looking down at our own faraway village basking in the winter sunlight.

We soon recovered our breath and ran to our favourite spots, each of us checking our sun-clocks. This kind of "clock" was the first watch I ever had.

On the mountain slope, we cleared away dead leaves leaving flat circles of bare earth about two feet across. In the middle of each circle we stuck a straight stick, which made a shadow on the ground. Each day we marked the shadow's position with a short stick and the next day went to check our time of arrival. "Earlier than yesterday!" or "Hurrah!"——shouts like these echoed around. If my shadow was even the tiniest bit to the west of yesterday's mark, it meant I was a little earlier today, and I put in another stick at the new place to look at the next day. If I made better time than the day before, I was always happy.

Far below, I sometimes saw my father and mother, like small beans, working in the fields, and sometimes we saw smoke coming from every roof-chimney. Lunch was cooking!

The Crying Mountain still stands behind our house. Looking up at it, I remember the pain, and the joy, of those times.

What kind of Crying Mountain will I have in my future life? I may have a hard slope to climb with bitter tears. But I must always remember the bright slope at the top where I have my own sun-clock; and from there I can see both sides of the mountain ridge——which I have climbed up and down and where I will walk in the future.

MY FATHER

It happened last year.

Some calyx hydrangeas stood in a vase on the table. Looking at them my father said:

"Soon all the buds will open and they'll look more beautiful." He seemed to think that calyx hydrangeas are the same as ordinary ones.

"No, Dad," I said, "the small grains in the middle will stay like that. Those are *calyx* hydrangeas, different from common ones."

"Wait a bit more, and you'll see. Last year and the year before, each flower opened wide like a ball."

He was full of confidence. The drink he had had at supper was having its strong effect. He is such a stubborn man that even when he finds he is wrong, once he has expressed an opinion he never changes it. Although he's a very dependable man, because of his strong will he has sometimes been a loser in the past.

Calyx hydrangeas flower in the centre of our garden each year. Every day he looked at those flowers. Hearing him speak with such confidence, I thought I must be mistaken and felt a bit down-hearted. But——a calyx hydrangea is a calyx hydrangea. All the family were on my side, so I made a bet with my father for the first time in my life.

CONTRACT

If the inside buds do not open like the outer flowers,
Father will pay Tomihiro ten thousand yen.

We made two copies. Father kept one and I the other. My mother, my brother and his wife were witnesses. At first my father, with great confidence, offered to pay several hundred thousand yen, but thinking I would never be able to receive such an unrealistic amount I decided that the stake would be just ten thousand yen.

By and by, summer passed into autumn. The long-flowering calyx hydrangeas began to lose their petals, but the flowers never became ball-shaped as my father had said they would, and finally they died. My father didn't say anything. I didn't ask him to pay up the bet. I thought that the dried brown hydrangeas would speak to him without words.

The following year——that means this spring——I heard from my bed the sound of pruning shears near the hydrangeas in the garden. That afternoon I went out into the garden in my wheel-chair and found several hydrangea bushes, which had been putting forth new green buds, cut down almost to the roots.

The hydrangea season has come again. Pale-purple flowers are blooming, apologetically somehow, on the narrow stems which escaped my father's hand....

Father was born in the Year of the Dragon, on 22nd March, 1904.

FRIEND

There's a song called *Rossalya in the Mountains*. I'm not sure, but maybe it's a Russian folk song. It's very beautiful, and whenever I hear it on the radio I'm always reminded of my close friend Mr. S.

The first time I saw him was at our primary school Entrance Ceremony. He was crying. Much later, when we were in the same class in our second year at Junior High School, we began to talk to each other. Once, we were singing in chorus in a music class with our teacher at the piano, when I suddenly realized that the person next to me was singing a different tune.

What a strange fellow, I thought, and as I listened, what a surpise! The words of the song were the same but his melody was quite different. At first I thought he was being cheeky and singing in a lower key, but then I remembered something I had forgotten: I had heard a rumour that Mr. S was completely tone-deaf.

After that, in every music class, I listened for the sound of his voice and swallowed back my laughter. Strangely though, we somehow became friends.

In the winter of our third year at Junior High School, one Sunday morning just before our high-school entrance examination, he and I climbed the highest mountain above our village, I with a pair of skis on my shoulder.

About seven miles from human habitation there was not a soul in sight, only silver birch trees, and it was utterly quiet.

My skis were very old like something in a museum, and his ski-boots had been given to him by his uncle. We had to take turns wearing the skis but we had a good time. Our style, however, was quite different from the brave feats we had imagined ourselves performing several days before.

We jumped head-first into the snow and made little cairns of stone. Time passed like a flash. We walked back along a forest path carved out of the side of a precipice. The sun was low in the sky, but I didn't want to go back——because when we returned the entrance exam would be waiting for me.

We were both taking the exam for only one high school. According to my school marks, there was only the very slightest possibility of my passing. If I failed, I'd have to stay at home and help my father on the farm. On the lonely mountain road, though I had to get back home quickly, my feet were heavy, as if they were tangled in a web of examinations. Just then, my friend asked me:

"Can you teach me how to sing *Rossalya in the Mountains*?"

"What?" I thought. "Mr. S? He wants to sing a song?" I was surprised. Since he'd become my close friend, I had never laughed at his singing. Instead, I felt deep sympathy for him when I heard him sing in a small voice during his music examination.

To sing songs is a terrifying ordeal for him, I thought, yet such a fellow wants me to teach him one. He wanted me to teach him *Rossalya in the Mountains*, which I was humming at the time, even though, he said, he was not much good at singing.

I started to sing it slowly, half in doubt. He also started to sing ——in a great loud voice I had never heard before.

I wish I could explain in words how beautifully his voice harmonized with the mountain valley. It was not so romantic——his voice was more like the howling of a wolf——yet it harmonized most uncannily with the murmur of the little stream far down below our feet at the foot of the precipice. But he sang; he sang the song again and again, joyfully and in time to the sound of our footsteps on the frozen ground.

The other day I went to the same place in my brother's car. The sheer cliff and the sound of the stream hadn't changed at all. I couldn't believe that twenty years had passed since then——even though I thought of all the things that had happened in that space of time.

On the way back, again, as before, the sun was low in the sky. The car turned a corner close to the rocks, and I couldn't help imagining that before my very eyes I saw the backs of me and my friend, walking there and singing *Rossalya in the Mountains*.

Just as he had hoped to be at that time, Mr. S is now a news-reporter.

SPRING

As I watch the mountains putting forth new leaves and dressing themselves in fresh verdure, I feel a sense of overabundance in the passing of time.

I always have the same feeling in this season; but that's an old story....

In my university days, I used to go up to the rooftop of the building with a roll of bread wrapped in a paper bag.

I used to gaze at the three great mountains of Gunma covered with their fresh green, until it was time to go to my club activity.

I never got tired of gazing at the same view day after day....

On the Joshu plain that has produced many poets like Sakutaro Hagiwara and Bocho Yamamura and so on, I stood there absorbing the poetic atmosphere——or rather, I wish I could say I was. The fact is, it wasn't like that at all. Without my realizing it, the springtime of my life was passing away, and I was eating my melon-flavoured bread bit by bit, feeling a sense of wastefulness as the fresh green of the trees deepened into thick foliage.

It's the same now, today and yesterday. I gaze at the mountains of my home town as I drive past the rice-fields in my electric wheel-chair.

Mountains I can see through a bamboo forest; mountains reflected in the water of the rice-plant nursery; mountains above the roof-tiles; mountains beyond gravestones....

In broad daylight, an adult is gazing at the mountains, and sighing ....in the busiest season for farmers....

It's too much of a luxury. I can't say in public how small I feel. If I keep this beautiful scenery in mind, I suppose one day in the future I can express it in a painting or essay.

I'm sure I've become stronger since I started painting pictures. Of course, I seek for beautiful things as much as I can. Since I took up my weapon——this painting brush——I am moved to do quite willingly even the most difficult things, things that I used to run away from....

I was outside all day today until it began to get dark. I caught the smell of tempura cooking somewhere and without meaning to turned back home.

Even inside the house, I gazed at the mountains from the window ....a view that I never get tired of....

In the garden, red and purple azaleas are in full bloom....

White smoke floats like a thread from the back garden where someone is boiling bamboo shoots....

To me the mountains look like a huge black folding screen.

I can hear the voice of the mountain cuckoo——as if it is tapping with its beak on the bole of a bamboo-tree——mixed with the croaking of frogs....

THE ORCHID RETURNS

The first time I saw a live orchid was when I was in hospital.

On the first Sunday of every month, a pastor visited me for Holy Communion, bringing sacramental bread and wine——because I couldn't go to Church myself.

On one occasion, another man came with the pastor. His name was Nishio and he was carrying an orchid with a long stalk in his hand like a stick.

Till that time, I had never seen an actual orchid, although I'd heard its name many times and imagined it must be a very beautiful flower. Mr. Nishio said:

"I've built a greenhouse and grow orchids for a hobby."

He put it on my bedside table and I took a long look at it. It was a Cymbidium variety and much more beautiful than I expected.

Just as Mr. Nishio said——"It'll keep like this for about a month"——the orchid continued to bloom near my face week after week.

Looking at it every day, I thought: "Even a long-lived flower has to die——sooner or later." Wishing somehow to preserve its beauty, I tried to paint a picture of it. It took me a long time. I knew my picture was no match for the real thing, but at least, I thought, I could keep the deep emotion it inspired in me.

Though I say it myself, to my mind that painting is surprisingly good. I thought I'd like to present it to Mr. Nishio as a token of gratitude.

Incidentally, a certain Miss Watanabe used to visit me regularly every Saturday after leaving her office. These visits continued for more than two years.

Whatever pictures I painted——even small ones or bad ones——she alway asked me to show them to her. She looked at each one for a long time with a kind of amazement in her eyes.

"Beautiful," she said with admiration. "Superb!"

I showed my orchid painting to Miss Watanabe. She was overwhelmed with surprise and deeply moved, so I said to her lightly:

"This isn't such a good painting, but if you can bear to have it, I'll give it to you."

Because of this, the orchid painting which I ought to have presented to Mr. Nishio I suddenly gave to Miss Watanabe. Mr. Nishio was nearly sixty, Miss Watanabe a charming young lady. I wonder what made me change my mind....!

At first, she told me, she fastened the picture with selotape on the wall above her desk. Gradually, however, she began to feel it was of special significance and so she had it framed....and in the end, she became....my bride, bringing the painting with her....

*

The priest who conducted our wedding ceremony was Funaki the pastor; the go-between was Mr. Nishio——the same two who had come to the hospital to perform the Communion service....bringing the orchid. In his speech as go-between, Mr. Nishio said:

"If I may say so, it was not me but a flower that acted as go-between in this love affair...." He pointed to my painting of the orchid as he spoke.

I felt sorry that I had not given the painting to Mr. Nishio, but what I did do was the best thing that could have happened.

In April, 1981, along with the bridal dowry, my dear old orchid painting returned to me....

EPILOGUE

About this time last year I wrote the epilogue of my previous book *Love—From an Abyss*——gazing at the autumn-tinted mountains from the window as now.

I felt a contradiction. I wanted many people to read my book, but at the same time I felt ashamed of letting people read it. Beyond this small dilemma, however, not only in Japan but also among Japanese people overseas, my book was wildly acclaimed, and during this last ten months I have received more than two thousand, five hundred heart-warming letters from them.

I have often been moved by reading other people's books, but I have never had the courage to write to the authors.

Considering my situation, I am full of gratitude to all those who have written to me. One thing has worried me very much, however. I have been unable to answer almost all the letters. Thinking of many ways how I might do this, I came to the conclusion that the best way of answering them was, by continuing to paint pictures to the best of my ability, to publish this book of paintings, poems and essays.

Some of the poems have already appeared in my first book, but originally each poem was written after I had painted a picture. Now, after a long separation, poems and paintings are restored to their proper place.

Some of the paintings are no longer in my possession. After an absence of several years, I met my own paintings again, just like old friends who had shared my hardships of the past. It felt like having a class-reunion meeting with my own flowers.

The painting of rape-blossoms is part of a letter I wrote to my niece in Yokohama five years ago. I wrote the words of this letter very close to the picture itself. Other paintings have appeared as a series in the magazine *Some Day Somewhere*, and some of them are new paintings which I've made during the last two years.

It seems very strange to me, however, that I can publish my own books. Before my injury, I was living in a world quite without paintings or words.... Furthermore, I can't use my hands to hold a brush or pen, but in spite of that I'm painting and writing now.

I cannot help thinking that all this is due to the fact that I cannot use brush or pen in the usual way. Until my injury, I took the ability to paint and write too much for granted, and I didn't realize what a wonderful thing it is. When natural things became unnatural, so to speak, I learned how wonderful each actual letter is, how delightful it is to be able to write and how marvellous it is to be able to paint pictures.

Flowering plants, the love of human beings, the works of God——I was amazed to rediscover all these things around me. I noticed that I too had been given life the same as all these beautiful things.

I cannot move my body except to turn my neck or shake my head a little. But that is no problem at all: I can leave my footprints on life's journey. Grasses and leaves of trees waving in the wind have told me that.

I would love to reach out for field weeds at the edge of the path without thinking about it.

I would love to blow the seeds off a dandelion clock.

At such times, the breeze blows gently over the fields and touches my cheek.

I send my mind into the spirit of the wind. I stroke the petals of flowers and fly high in the sky with the seeds of dandelions. I rustle through the ears of corn, turning the leaves the other way one by one. I climb up the green mountain....

However hard I try to paint, I cannot grasp the beauty of the original things; but from now on, I will continue painting, and as long as I have in my mind the ability to be surprised and the capacity to be moved in my heart, I cannot help painting in the future.

Before closing, let me say this: I have been able to discover what I can do, and I could do that because the doctors and nurses of Gunma University Orthopaedic Hospital took care of my body for nine long years. I am deeply in debt to them and to Dr. Ushikubo who has visited me often since I came back home; also to Mr. Minoru Kubota and Mr. Tadashi Saito, and to Mrs. Sonoko Yamazaki and Miss Atsuko Kono of Rippu Shobo, who helped with the publication of this book; and, without naming names, to everybody in Maebashi Church of Christ, and to all the people who have supported me. I am grateful to you all.

10 November, 1981   TOMIHIRO HOSHINO

TRANSLATORS' NOTE

It has been a great pleasure for us to translate these poems and essays and to enable English-speaking people to appreciate the beautiful and sensitive thoughts of Mr. Hoshino.

In order not to allow footnotes to mar the simple lay-out of each page, we feel that perhaps a few explanations are necessary. As for the poems, virtually no punctuation is used in poetry of this kind, so we also have used very little. The lines are arranged so as to bring out the sense as exactly as possible and to convey the "floating" quality of the images and ideas.

The names of some of the flowers present a few difficulties. Certain of the flowers can be found only in Japan or as Japanese variants. We have used English names which approximate as nearly as possible to these, but in certain cases, because we wanted to avoid using Latin or botanical terms, we have "coined" new ones. For example, *Thorn Flower* on page 11 is really *Euphorbia Millii*, in some countries known as Thorn Spurge. On page 26, the Japanese name of the plant is *dokudami*, the literal meaning of which is "poison-gatherer". It is used as a poultice to draw poison from septic spots. For this reason, we have called the poem *Poultice Flowers*. *Mother's-Heart* on page 32 is another name for Shepherd's Purse. We have used the former as being more pertinent to the poem. *Giant Spider Plant* on page 41 is called in Japanese *fucho-so*, the literal translation of which is "wind-bird-grass", but the flower itself looks something like the burst of a firework or sparkler (known in Japanese as *hana-bi*——"flower-fire"). It is this image which inspires Mr. Hoshino's poem. *Cat's Bauble* on page 43 is a near-literal translation of the Japanese name of the flower *neko-jarashi*——"cat's plaything", a larger variety of which is known as Green Bristlegrass.

The literal Japanese for Gardenia (on page 9) is *kuchi-nashi* which means "no mouth"——because the fruit of this plant, unlike some which open out when mature, seems to have no mouth. Mr. Hoshino gives the poem a humorous touch by using the word "mouth" in the last line.

The complexity of the Chinese characters (*kanji*) mentioned in *Butterburs* (on page 18) can be seen in the original poem, which is printed on page 49.

On page 59, "a lady snake——more than beautiful with her head one twentieth of her total length" needs explanation. In Japan, a woman is nowadays regarded as ideally beautiful if her head measures one eighth of her total height. The Yagi-bushi Bon-dance mentioned on page 59 is a local folk-dance of Gunma Prefecture, held in August during the Buddhist Bon Festival——during which people visit their family graves. On page 60, the "*taro*-potatoes" are the sticky potato-like vegetable known variously as "tara", "dalo", "tansheen" or "elephant's ear".

Dayflower on page 38 can only be properly understood if one remembers that Mr. Hoshino's mother spent nine years taking care of her son in hospital before he came back to live at home and she could return to her farming and gardening work.

One last mention should perhaps be made about the pronunciation of various proper names. The final -*se* of "Watarase" (p.54)and -*be* of "Miss Watanabe" (p.70) are both pronounced with the "e" sound as in "send" and "bend".

We are deeply grateful to all those who have helped to make the publication of this translation possible.

Kyoko and Gavin Bantock
July, 1987

TOMIHIRO HOSHINO

The life of Tomihiro Hoshino stands as a shining example of human courage, endurance and cheerful optimism. The way he has lived, and the way he lives now, teach us of the amazing resources, untapped by most of us, that reside in the human mind and body. When faced with misfortune ourselves, we can be inspired and encouraged by the way Mr. Hoshino met his hardships squarely in the face and overcame even the most unbearable of difficulties.

He was born on April 24, 1946, in the small mountain village of Azuma in Gunma Prefecture, north-east of Tokyo in the Japanese main island of Honshu. He led an active life enjoying various sports, gymnastics and mountain-climbing. After graduating from Gunma University, he became a gymnastics teacher in Kuragano Junior High School in Takasaki City, Gunma Prefecture. On June 17, 1970, only two months after beginning work, he had a serious accident while demonstrating a double somersault in the school gymnasium and became totally paralyzed from the neck down.

He then spent nine years in Gunma University Orthopaedic Hospital. During this period, he suffered extreme hardship. All he could do while lying motionlessly on his back was gaze at the ceiling; sometimes, because of respiratory and other bodily problems, he came perilously near to death, and at times he almost gave up in despair and wanted to die. Slowly, however, his physical condition improved and, strongly encouraged by his endlessly patient mother, and by his doctors, nurses, and friends, and also by the example of other patients, he recovered his mental composure. One day, in 1972, a young patient who had been transferred to another hospital sent his old canvas beach hat to Hoshino's ward, asking the patients there to write something on it for him. After painstaking efforts and with the help of his mother, Hoshino, holding a pen in his mouth, managed to write the first part of his name——"Tomi". This was a turning point. From that time on, he gradually learned how to write with his mouth and then to paint pictures. Slowly developing this technique, he eventually produced his first flower picture and his first poems. Step by step, these blossomed out into hundreds, and he has continued such artistic endeavours with great success ever since. He has now published several illustrated books of poems and essays and a number of exhibitions of his paintings have been held.

He became a Christian in December, 1974, and married in April, 1981.

The writings and paintings of Mr. Hoshino stand as superb works of art in themselves. There is no need whatever for us to regard them as the products of a handicapped man, nor should we allow emotions of sympathy or admiration to stand in the way of our natural appreciation of these works as purely artistic creations.

GAVIN BANTOCK
July, 1987

PHOTO BY KOEI IIJIMA

NOTE ON THE ENGLISH VERSION

高校時代の 英語の試験では、よく 3点 とか 5点 とか
とったものです。 もちろん 100点 満点 でです。
横文字 恐怖症は かなり 重症でしたが、バントック夫妻の
英訳にかける 熱い思いに、ずいぶん軽くなった気がします。
バントック夫妻に心から感謝します。
なお、この本に使っている絵は、日本語版「風の旅」
とは多少異なります。 たび重なる展覧会の強い照明
のために 原画の色が褪せてしまい、色を塗り足したり
描きかえたものも あるのです。御了承下さい。

星野富弘

In my high-school days, I never used to get more than three or five marks out of a hundred in my English examinations. I developed a rather serious "foreign-language complex".

Now, however, because of the enthusiasm shown by Mr. and Mrs. Bantock in the making of this English translation of my book, my "phobia" seems to be melting away.

I wish to express my sincere thanks to them both from the bottom of my heart.

In addition, I feel I should explain that some of the pictures which appear in this English version are a little different from those in the Japanese version. The original paintings have been exhibited so many times that their colouring has faded due to exposure to strong light. I have therefore repainted or added some extra colour to some of them. I ask my readers' kind understanding about this.

by TOMIHIRO HOSHINO

JOURNEY OF THE WIND

First English Translation published in 1988
by Rippu Shobo Company
5-5-8, Kami-meguro, Meguro-ku, Tokyo 153, Japan

Original Japanese Version published in 1982
by Rippu Shobo Company

Book Designed by SHO SHIROTA

Edited by SONOKO YAMAZAKI

Printed in Japan
by Tosho Insatsu Company

ISBN4-651-11014-2 C0092